BIZARRO

by Dan Piraro

Chronicle Books • San Francisco

To my wife, Kalin, my daughter Killian and Bill

ISBN: 0-87701-402-7
10 9 8 7 6 5 4 3 2

Distributed in Canada by
Raincoast Books
112 East 3rd Avenue
Vancouver, B.C. V5T 1 C8

Chronicle Books
275 Fifth Street
San Francisco, CA 94103

Rudy Spaglio was a big man . . . But his wife was even bigger.

In India, gurus walk slowly across beds of hot peppers. Some people confuse these with hot coals which would, of course, burn your feet.

"Yes, sir! A ceiling fan is definitely the way to go in a big room like this."

"I've finally done it, Martha! Notify the papers and I'll meet you at the river!"

5

"Excuse me, sir . . . you'll have to cover your shirt, it's distracting the pitcher."

I JUST WANNA KNOW ONE THING! WHAT KEEPS YOU MOUNTIES GOING!

SOMETHING *YOU'LL* NEVER UNDERSTAND, JACQUES! A COMMITMENT TO *TRUTH* AND *JUSTICE*! AND UNLIMITED SNO-CONES WHEN WE GET BACK TO THE LODGE. . . .

"...and now, I proudly present you with the 'key to the city'...no long distance calls and don't forget to lock up when you leave."

"Behold! A new land ... where every man can forge his own future, be free to pursue happiness in an atmosphere of justice and equality for all humanity! ... Get rid of the locals and we'll be all set."

"There's a bull outside who can't remember if he's from that beer company or that investment company. Can he use the phone?"

Though Steve had no real friends to speak of, he threw numerous cocktail parties. Lenora was his favorite guest.

"I just walked a mile in your shoes, Dad,
and it was no picnic."

"It's okay, Ralph. We'll be safe in here."

DuBois dives, LaSalle blocks,
the lintballs remain in place and the
whiskbroom competition goes on.

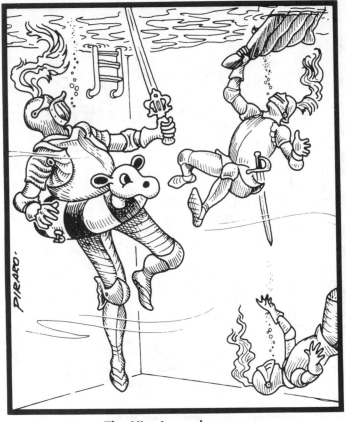

The King's pool party.

10

Jasper likes a good rare steak

"Hi there! We're George and Donna, your neighbors from across the street and we were wondering when you're going to take down your Christmas lights."

"Well . . . . OK. But just be careful."

12

"Well, yes it's sturdy, but the squirrels downstairs have been complaining and the kids haven't slept in weeks!"

"But I HAVE to go to work, don't be silly...
I'll be home this evening and we'll read the
paper together just like always."

Moms Against Mimes.

15

"We'd better get started, sir!
The press conference is in four hours!"

It had taken a tad longer
than they had first imagined.

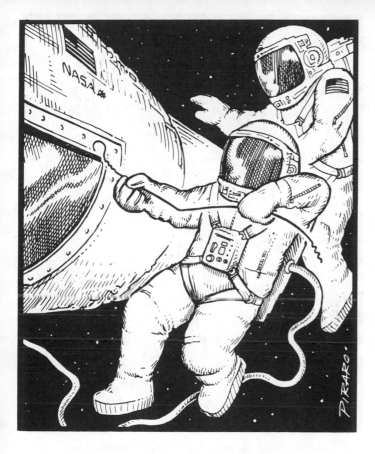

"'See Spot. See Spot run. See Spot run and play...' What IS this garbage?"

19

It was another frantic day at the New York sock exchange.

The endless search for my real parents was full of false alarms and disappointments.

"They're cute when they're that age, aren't they?"

"The enemy has been making fun of our hats again, Colonel. And frankly, some of the men are having second thoughts about them too."

22

**Ancient rodent monument unearthed during
construction project in Egypt.**

**"So what's somebody like you doing out on
a day like this without an umbrella?"**

23

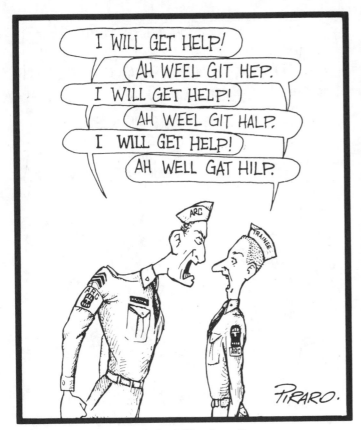

Accent Rehabilitation Camp

Charlie on Merv.

26

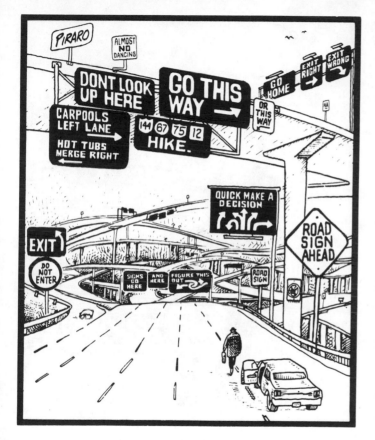

27

"I'd like to get the other half of my barbell
set out of layaway, please."

The bullies of Julliard.

"Excuse me sir! Do you have change for a dollar? Miss? Do you have change for... Hey, little boy! Hey you!..."

"Where have you been? Billy fell over again, help me pick him up! And get that animal out of the house! What IS it, anyway?

"I don't feel good about this, Jake...."

"That does it, Marlene! Now I KNOW I'm shrinking."

**PLEASE, Darrell! It's not worth it!
Just give him the ants, Darrell! PLEASE!"**

"I'm bored, Steven. If we don't get out of this rut we're in, I think I'll lose my mind."

"One more step and you're a dead cowboy."

"CHARGE it?" I wouldn't use it for a bathrobe!"

"Hey, Roy, check out the majestic looking
redhead ..."

I remember all too well the day
Mr. Coffee walked out of my life.

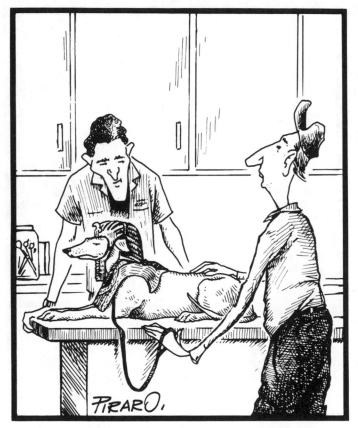

"At first, we thought it was real cute,
Dr. Murray. But now he says he won't take it
off 'till we answer some dumb riddle, and
me and the Mrs. are stumped.!"

"D'you like 'em?"

Yellowstone

"Dr. Simms, you are this year's recipient of the coveted 'Albert G. Thompson Award'. And here, for your personal enrichment for one full year, is Albert G. Thompson."

"Oh, well . . . It was a nice thought."

38

"Oh, sure, we get a little high water
from time to time but we've lived all over
this valley. It's beautiful!"

"Ladies and gentlemen of the city council:
Observe, if you will, my proposal for the
Monument to Big Business! Yours for only
29 million tax dollars."

By and large,
the experiment went undetected.

"I don't KNOW how it happened, Lucy. Just call security!"

41

The art of censorship.

"All right, who had the
Warhol Luncheon Special?"

"Time out!! . . .
There's nobody in Jackson's uniform!"

"Hi, dear, put on these 3-D glasses, have a seat and let me tell you about my day..."

The troublemaker.

Thesaurus Rex

Military induction procedure on Mars.

"Yellow, yellow, yellow! I'm SICK of it! There's
a lovely apartment upstairs all done in red.
Can't we move?"

"You and that newspaper! I don't guess you noticed I rearranged the furniture today ..."

"Someone's put a speed bump on that last curve."

Snookem's bath night.

Peter Pan made a fortune in tips after he retired from show business.

"Hey, Mom, can you help my new friend,
Rusty, tie his shoe?"

The latest trend: High fashion honesty.

"Stop worrying, Sophie!
They're a lower species, they don't feel
things the way we do."

54

"Careful, lieutenant. This could be a trap."

"Mind if I smoke?"

The company picnic.

56

"OK, I'll give you the promotion, Ms. Burke!
Just wave him off!"

When wrestlers go shopping.

"Hate the slacks, love the sweater."

Agonies of the rich and famous.

The chess shark.

A night at the opera.

Metaphysical State University

Joke tobacco was a favorite trick at the Boston Avenue Gentlemen's Club.

"Have a wonderful time on your vacation, Mr. Crosby. I'll be taking over for you while you're gone."

"Hand over the cash or I'll mail this
icky fish without a zipcode!"

65

"At the sound of the tone,
the time will be eleven thirty-three.
Temperature, seventy-eight."

"...so the female iguana really goes
for this, huh?"

"You don't give 'em much to aim at,
do ya kid?"

67

America's love affair with
the full-size sedan.

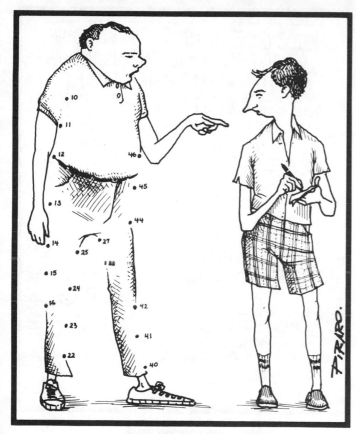

"Say there, bub.
Can I borrow your pen a second?"

Aunt Ruby did some of her best surveillance
work while wearing her brick print dress.

"My life in a nutshell: Peanut butter and jelly in my wallet . . . money in my sandwich . . . but not enough to go out to lunch."

Neptune's manicurist.

A popular rural American
sideshow attraction.

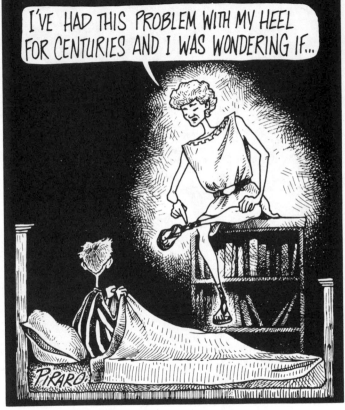

Achilles appears in a vision to a young Dr. Scholl.

73

The fourth in a series.

Suddenly it was all very clear. Life would be a series of great disappointments followed by minor windfalls.

"You WISH ..."

"Take whatever you want but PLEASE don't hurt us anymore!"

The Franco-Spanish border dispute of 1680.

M. C. Escher and his dog, Lydia

"This I wrested from a Byzantine soldier . . . .
These are from the pillage of Burgundy . . . .
This cometh from a Prussian warrior . . . and
THIS from a two-tone Buick LaSabre."

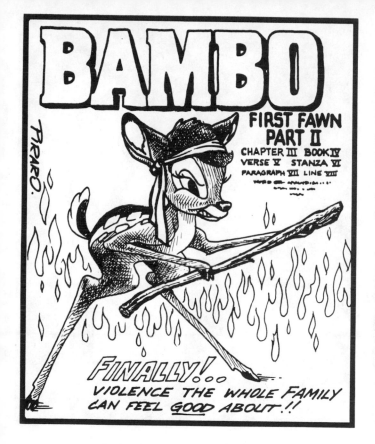

"Perhaps THIS will refresh your memory!!"

"Good morning, Jack. Your eggs are in the skillet, coffee's almost done and, of course, WE'RE ready when you are."

The Bnona sisters are trained and skilled professionals. Don't try this at home.

"To tell you the truth, it's got me stumped.
Fortunately, I keep a hieroglyphics expert on
staff at all times ... BILLY RAY!!!"

"Someone should be with you folks in
a few minutes ..."

"Is this the 'How to Detect Consumer Fraud' course? ... Hello?"

86

"It's quite a problem, really.
I'm EXTREMELY superstitious but I just can't
abide cruelty to animals."

The trouble with the barter system.

"I'm not going in that bank 'till he tucks the feet in!"

90

"A lightning rod, Greg? You let that stupid skin diver sell you a lightning rod!?"

"Now remember, Aunt Ira and Uncle Jack are a little primitive, but they're very nice, so behave yourself . . . and no cracks about the dog, either!"

Chapter 20, page 254. General Maysky is captured.

"Run, Frosty! Run!"

"I opened up the sleeper sofa today and found $.39 in change and this old house guest."

"Tell Moby we're ready when he is."

Championship rustling.

"Years ago, I used to chase these little rascals all over the place. Now, I just wait till they come up for the walnuts and nab 'em."

100

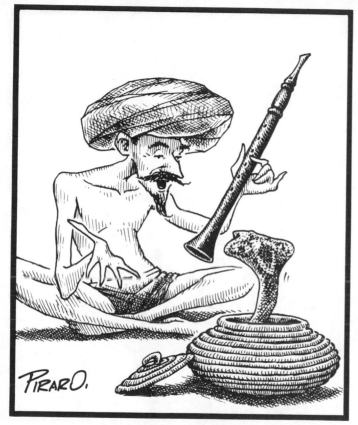

"Here's the deal . . . You don't bite me and I won't beat you senseless with this flute, OK?"

"A recent survey shows that kids prefer 'grandmom's chicken noodle soup' over the leading brand of laundry detergent or this aspirin-free cold remedy!"

101

"So this is the Nobel prize....
Somehow I always thought it would be money,
or a plaque or something."

"Wallace! Stop trying to be something
you're not!"

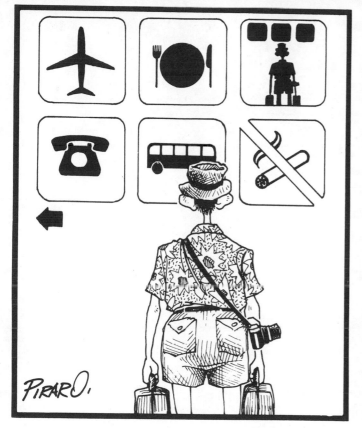

Shameful as it is, there are no laws governing the way doctors dress on their day off.